TERMINOLOGY FOR THE

WORLD OF

LITHOGRAPHY

Terminology
For The
World
of
Lithography

PPC Publications

Whitman, MA

Manufactured in the United States of America

ACKNOWLEDGEMENTS

This book has been made possible by PPC Publications with the assistance of the advertisers contained within and the following manufacturers:

Typesetting:	*American Typesetting, Inc.*
Color Separation and Film Preparation:	*Pre-Press Co., Inc.*
Text & Cover Printing:	*Diversified Printing Services Co., Inc.*
Paper:	*Roosevelt Paper Company*
Finishing:	*New England Book Components, Inc.*
Binding:	*Heffernan Inc.*
Packaging:	*NEV Industrial Services*
Cover Photo:	*Comstock, Inc.*

It is our hope that this book will assist many in their quest for lithographic knowledge.

It's easy to solve the puzzle when you make all the pieces.

We built the finest graphic arts system piece by piece. We started with film: Grandex, then FineLite and now our new, HG Series Self-Cleaning Film. Then we added PS-Plates. The most complete aqueous plate line available, anywhere. To deliver the most consistent, high-quality color proofing, we introduced Color-Art which satisfies the most critical color manager. All processed with our chemistry and with our equipment. For the finest monotone scanning, we introduced the Scanart 450II. Our AP 5000 Color Copier also offers unequaled reproduction. Put it all together with our phototypesetting film and paper and reprographic copiers and supplies, and you'll discover we've got the graphic arts down to a system.

FUJI FILM
A New Way of Seeing Things

Abba *(in printing)* — a term used to indicate stepping a quad insert imposition on a plate.

Accordian Fold — parallel folds of two or more that open like an accordian.

Additive Primaries — a white light produced by combining red, green, and blue light.

Against The Grain — paper being folded or fed at right angles to the paper grain.

Agate Line — a measurement standard for the column depth of advertising space (14 "agate" lines equal one column inch).

Airbrush — in order to correct or produce tone or graduated tonal effects a small pencil-like pressure gun is used to spray watercolor pigment using compressed air.

Alpha Channel — an 8-bit channel saved in some programs to use for masking or adding color information.

Alterations — changes to the copy after typesetting is completed.

Anti-aliasing — blending hard objects smoothly into a background or combining object-like art with bit maps.

Antique Finish — the term describing a paper which has a natural rough finish.

Artifact — a visible defect in an image caused by inadequate hardware or software.

Ascender — the part of a letter rising above the base, as in "d".

ASCII — the abbreviated form of: **A**merican **S**tandard **C**ode **F**or **I**nformation **I**nterchange — in specified form for listing digital info in 8-bit chunks.

Backbone — the section against the back of a book between the front and back cover.

Backing Up *(in printing)* — to print on the back of a sheet which is already printed.

Backing Up *(in electroplating)* — a copper shell being backed with metal to meet required thickness.

Back Lining — the paper or fabric glued to the backbone or spine on a casebound book.

Bad Break — a hyphenated line set as the first line of a page or a "widow."

Banding — a visible ascending or descending of shades.

Basis Weight — the pound weight of 500 sheets (a ream) of paper cut to a standard size for the particular grade, i.e. a ream (500 sheets) of 25x38, 80 lb. coated paper will always weigh 80 pounds.

Bearers — the ends of the cylinders which make contact during printing determining the packing thickness required.

Bezier Curves — the shape of a curve indicated by anchor points placed along the arc in object oriented programs.

Bimetal Plate — a plate which has copper or brass in the image area and aluminum, stainless steel, or chromium in the non-printing area; used for printing long runs.

Bit — a binary digit or the littlest unit of information in a computer.

Bitmapped — a rectangular grid of pixels forming an image. Each pixel has a value assigned by the computer from one bit (black & white) to 24 bits per pixel for full color.

Black and White — text or illustration in a single color rather than multi-color.

Blanket — a fabric with a rubber surface that is mounted on the press cylinder that transfers the images from the plate to the paper.

Bleed — a page with the image extending off the trim edge of the sheet to insure complete coverage.

Blind Embossing — a bas-relief effect produced by stamping a design without goldleaf or ink.

Blind Image — an image that will no longer hold ink.

Blowup — to increase the size.

Blueprint — a proof made from a negative to show how the printed image will look.

Body — the consistency or viscosity of an ink — an ink with too much body is stiff.

Body Type — to indicate the type size to be used for the text part of a page.

Bold Face Type — the heavier type that is used versus a text-size type.

Bond Paper — a grade of paper with strength and durability.

Book Paper — coated or uncoated papers in the basic size of 25x38.

Box Size — size of page before final trim.

Break For Color — to distinguish the different colors to be printed (in the artwork or composition).

Brightness *(in photography)* — reflection of light by the copy.

Brightness *(in paper)* — reflection or brilliance by the paper.

Brochure — a booklet form of a pamphlet.

Bronzing — producing a metallic lustre by applying bronze powder to a sizing ink while still wet.

Bulk — the number of pages per inch based on the basis weight and paper thickness.

Byte — a term describing 8 bits of digital data, used to measure or describe a file size such as megabyte, kilobyte, and gigabyte.

Camera-Ready Art — any text or artwork which is ready to be shot on camera.

Calibration — using a standard measure to properly set equipment.

Calendar Rolls — horizontal cast-iron rolls which paper goes through at the end of a paper machine to add smoothness and gloss.

Caliper — thickness of paper by the thousandths of an inch (mils).

Caps and Small Caps — two different sizes of capital letters in one type style — usually roman.

Case — a hard-bound book cover.

Cast Coated — a coated paper with a high-gloss enamel finish produced by drying it under pressure on a polished cylinder.

Catching Up — the scumming or non-taking of ink on the non-image area of a press-plate.

Chalking — improperly dried ink which causes the pigment to dust off because it has been absorbed too quickly by the paper.

Coated Paper — paper with a smooth finish produced by a surface coating. The surface can range from eggshell to glossy.

Cold Color — a color in printing that tends to look bluish.

**At Diversified,
it's not just how hard we work,
it's how much we <u>accomplish.</u>**

Control

At Diversified, we're pushing back the limits of printing and graphic production. When you have one shot at a production deadline, you must be able to manage and regulate every specification. At Diversified, we're in control.

Full-Range of Services

- Prompt Response
- Personal Attention
- Rapid Turnaround
- State-of-the-Art Equipment
- Design & Art Services
- Camera & Pre-Press Departments
- Complete Finishing & Binding Facilities

72 Sharp Street ▪ Hingham, MA 02043 ▪ Telephone (617) 335-8990 ▪ FAX (617) 335-9119

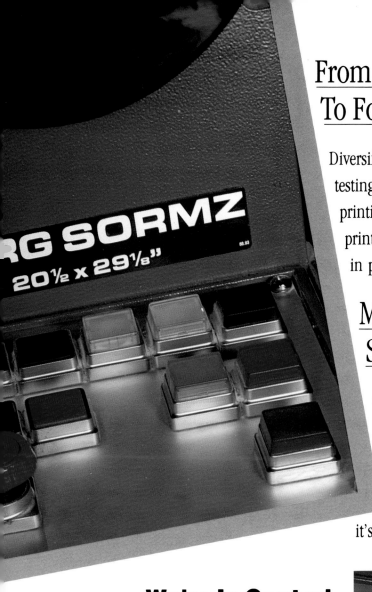

From Breakthrough To Follow-Through

Diversified leads the way in testing and evaluating new printing technology. To us, printing is a new dimension in personal performance.

Making A Significant Mark

Satisfied and repeat customers can attest to the fact that it's not just how hard we work, it's how much we accomplish.

We're In Control

DIVERSIFIED
PRINTING SERVICES CO., INC.

1-800-439-8991

Collate — sheets or signatures being gathered in sequence during the binding process.

Color Art® — an accurate color proofing system by Fuji Photo Film USA, Inc. using colored acetate layers combined to replicate the final product.

Color Correction — improving color by any method, i.e. scanning, dot-etching, re-touching.

Color Correction *(in desktop publishing)* — the adjustment of an image to make up for scanner inabilities or to allow for deficiencies in the computer output.

Color Filter — glass plates used on cameras containing gelatin, or dyed gelatin, dyed glass or plastic to absorb difficult colors or to obtain better results on others.

Color Picker — a device enabling the choosing of certain colors on the computer monitor.

Color Proofs *(in 4 color scanning or desktop)* — a proof with all colors combined to show what the printed piece will look like.

Color Proofs — proofs made from the separate film in process work to show how the printed item will look with the colors together.

Color Separation *(in photography)* — negatives or positives in the primary colors obtained from full color originals or transparencies with a separate piece of film for each color.

Color Separation *(in lithographic platemaking)* — colors manually separated during the stripping process.

Color Transparency — a 35mm color slide or larger color transparent film.

Combination — combining multiple positives or negatives into single-piece film by contacting.

Contact Print — a paper print of an image or text made by a negative or positive being contacted with sensitized paper under pressure.

Condensed Type — a typeface which is slender or narrow.

Continuous Tone — an unscreened photographic image containing gradated tones from black and white.

Contrast — the difference between the lightest and darkest areas of a photograph.

Copy — the typewritten or typeset material, pictures, or artwork used to produce negatives for offset printing.

Copyfitting — determining the amount of a particular size and style of type that can fit on a given area.

Copy Preparation — the paste-up or arrangement of text, halftones, or line illustrations in the desired location on the page to be photographed for offset printing.

Cover Paper — a basic term covering a wide selection of papers used for outside covers of books, brochures, catalogs, etc.

Creep — the moving of the blanket or the packing under the plate during printing.

Cromalin® — a color proofing system using powder pigments instead of ink put out by E. I. duPont de Nemours & Company, Inc.

Crop — the elimination of parts of a photograph or plate that is not wanted shown by placing ''crop marks'' on the original or proof.

Copyboard — the frame on a camera that holds the original copy while being photographed.

Crossmarks — used in printing for exact positioning of one color over another; illustration or halftone positioning with text; also known as register marks.

CT — letters indicating ''continuous tone''. A file which is used for the exchange of high-level scan data.

Curl — the concave side of a sheet of paper used in printing which has curled due to moisture absorption, or difference in the coating between the two sides.

Cut — a photoengraving of any kind on a letter press.

Cut-off — the length of print which measures the same as the plate cylinder's circumference.

Cylinder Gap — a space in the press cylinders where the plate clamps and grippers are located.

Dampeners — the rollers, usually cloth-covered or rubber, that dampen the press plate with a solution.

Dandy Roll — a wire cylinder which produces a woven or laid effect on the paper's texture.

DCS — a specific form which produces five post script files for each color image in desktop color separation.

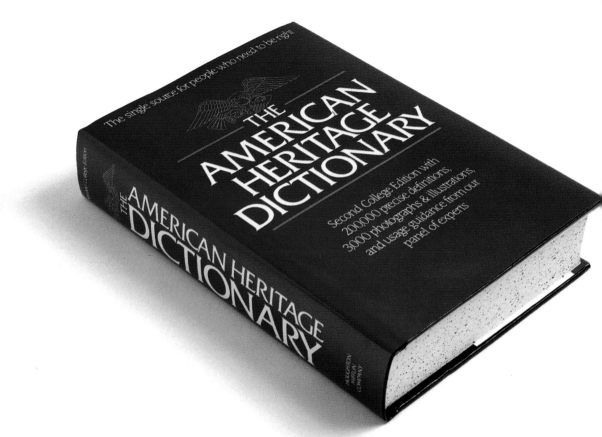

Here are 1568 pages that back us up.

Along with 3000 half tones and line illustrations.

When Houghton Mifflin Company needed film prepared for the American Heritage Dictionary, Second College Edition, they turned to Pre-Press Co., Inc.

Houghton Mifflin knows we have the right blend of experience, service and technology to handle the pre-press demands of one of America's most popular reference books.

Pre-Press has been serving magazine and book publishers for nearly 20 years. Our integrated capabilities provide everything necessary for superior reproduction—from in-house color separations, to proofing, to preparation of composite film ready for shipment to any printing facility in the U.S.

And when it comes to customer service, Pre-Press has no peer. Our sales and service representatives are experienced in all aspects of the pre-press process. They'll respond quickly to all your service needs, often providing quotations within hours.

So take a page out of Houghton Mifflin's book. If you're producing magazines, paperbacks, hard covers or textbooks of any kind, contact Pre-Press. We're *the* source for the pre-press services you need.

PRE-PRESS CO., INC.

356 South Avenue, Whitman, MA 02382, (617) 826-6526, FAX: (617) 447-4086.

Deckle — the width of the wet sheet of paper as it comes off the paper machine's wire.

Deckle Edge — the untrimmed paper edge that is feathery due to the flow of the pulp against the deckle.

Deep Etch — a positive-working plate on which the inked areas are recessed below the surface; usually used for long runs.

Densitometer *(in photography)* — an electric instrument used to determine the density of a photographic image or of colors.

Densitometer *(in printing)* — a reflection densitometer used to check the consistency of color density throughout the press run.

Density — a term used to indicate the relative blackening of a photographic image.

Descender — the section of a letter that extends below the main body, i.e. "y".

Desensitizer *(in lithographic platemaking)* — the chemical treatment of the non-image area of a plate to make it non-receptive to ink.

Densensitizer *(in photography)* — a substance used to make the development under comparatively bright light easier by decreasing the color sensitivity of the emulsion.

Developer — a chemical used in hand developing or in the processor which makes photo images visible after exposure to light.

Die-Cutting — the cutting of special shapes from printed sheets by using sharp steel rules; this can be done on either rotary or flat-bed presses.

Die-Stamping — copper or steel engraved with letters or designs used to print cards, letterheads by an intaglio process.

Dimensional Stability — the maintenance of size; paper or films resistence to size change due to an altering of relative humidity or moisture absorption.

Display Type — a type larger than the text used as an attention getter.

Dithering — the simulation of a third color in a bitmapped image by indicating specific color to adjacent pixels when a full color range is not available.

Dog Ear — a corner of a page folded over.

Dot — the element which produces the image of a halftone.

Dot Gain — an imperfection in printing which creates larger dots than intended creating darker colors or tones.

Dot Spread — the printing of dots larger than intended producing darker colors or tones.

Double Dot Halftone — one printing plate containing two halftone negatives combined, producing greater tonal range than a normal halftone; the highlights and shadows are produced by one negative while the middle tones are produced by the other. This is not the same as a duotone or printing with two black plates.

Drier — any product included or used to speed drying.

Drop-Out — colors or background areas that do not reproduce from a portion of the original copy — usually on purpose.

Drop Shipping — when a product is sent to a bulk mail center (BMC) or section center facility (SCF) in order to avoid zones which are farther away — saving money by the quantity shipment being nearer to its destination.

Dummy — a set of mock pages indicating the position of text and/or illustrations as they are to appear upon completion.

Duotone — a two-color halftone produced from one-color repro (copy).

Duplex Paper — a paper with each side having a different color or finish.

Duplicating Film — a lithographic film used to produce another negative or positive from the original film — can be used for line, halftone color separation.

Dylux® — a paper containing a blue element which is used for proofing — the images show in blue after the paper is exposed through film in a vacuum frame — manufactured by E.I. duPont de Nemours & Company, Inc.

Elliptical Dot — an elliptical shaped dot on a halftone screen which produces better gradation of tonal quality.

Em — the square body size of a piece of type — named for the square that the letter ''m'' used in early fonts.

Embossed Finish — a paper simulating wood, leather, cloth etc. accomplished by raising or depressing the surface.

Embossing — achieving a raised surface of an image by impressing over printing — blind embossing is done on blank paper.

Emulsion — a light-sensitive coating on film.

Emulsion Down — usually specified by the printer indicating that the readable image on the emulsion side faces away from the viewer.

En — one-half the square body size of an em.

English Finish — a more uniform, smoother paper grade than pages with a machine finish.

EPS — abbreviation for **E**ncapsulated **P**ost **S**cript. A specified file which transfers post script data from one program to another.

Errata — a list of errors loosely inserted into a book.

Etch *(in photoengraving)* — the use of chemical or electrolytic process to produce an image on a plate.

Etch *(in offset lithography)* — the use of an acid solution or acidified gum solution to desensitize the non-printing area of a plate and keep them ink free.

Extended Type — a type with a wider than normal width.

F&G — printed sheets which are folded and gathered prior to binding.

Face — a piece of type's printing area.

Facsimile — an exact copy of a letter, picture etc. The word is used in abbreviated form as ''fax.''

Feeder — the part of a press which feeds separate sheets in position for printing.

Felt Side *(in paper manufacturing)* — the top side of a sheet of paper.

Felt Side *(in printing)* — the smoothest side of paper.

Filling In — the filling in of ink in the area of spaces in type or between the dots in halftones.

Film — a thin sheet of cellulose material coated with a light-sensitive emulsion for making negatives.

Film Negative — a piece of film with dark areas clear and white areas black, (the opposite of a film positive).

Filter — a colored piece of gelatin used over or between the lens in black and white photography or color separation.

If you haven't received your new R.R. Bowker Catalog Call Today

R.R. BOWKER
Mailing List Rates & Data Catalog

Welcome to Bowker City!

A Division of Reed Publishing

Libraries/Librarians	36,09
School Library Journal	37,90
Library Journal	21,98
American Library Directory	36,09
Art/Graphic Arts	17,35
Book Trade	26,63
Politics	23,59
Science	104,65
Research & Technology	24,76
Publishers Weekly Magazine	29,66
Book Publishing U.S. Book Publishers	26,40
School Administrators District Personnel	276,40
School Market/ Principals	167,88
School Market/ Public Teachers	1,192,22
College Market	3,16

CAHNERS
THE WORLD OF LISTS AT WORK FOR YOU

249 West 17th Street   New York, NY 10011
212/337-7167   800/537-7930

To discuss your list needs,
Call John Panza at 800/537-7930.

Fixing — a chemical action to stabilize the image and prevent further exposure by removing unexposed silver halide.

Flash Exposure — an extra exposure in halftone photography in order to accentuate the shadow dots in a negative.

Flat *(in offset lithography)* — a composite of negatives or positives ready for plate-making — arranged in a certain order (imposition) for book or magazine printing.

Flat *(in photography)* — a picture lacking in contrast.

Flat-etching — reducing the silver deposit in a halftone or continuous-tone plate by submersing it in a chemical etching solution.

Flow — the capability of ink to cover the surface of printing press rollers.

Flush Cover -- a cover that is exactly the same size as the text pages.

Flush Left **(or right)** — type which lines up evenly at the left, or right, i.e. set type flush left.

Flush Paragraph — setting type with no indention for a new paragraph.

Flying Paster — an automatic paster which splices the end of one roll of paper onto a new roll (web) of paper while the press is running.

Fog — hazy density within the image on a negative.

Folio — the number of a text page.

Font — a complete set of type in a particular size and face.

Foot — the bottom of a page (i.e. foot margin is the space between the last line of type or folio and the bottom trim).

Form — a specific sequence of pages printed on both sides of one or more sheets of paper.

Form Rollers — the inking or dampening rollers which come in direct contact with the plate.

Format — the requirements of a printed piece in style, type, margins, printing, etc.

Fountain Solution — a solution of gum arabic, water and other chemicals which dampen the plate to keep non-printing area from printing.

Four Color Process — a wide range of colors produced by using the four primary colors of cyan (blue), magenta (red), yellow and black.

Free Sheet — paper that is manufactured without wood pulp.

"F" Stops — mechanism to determine amount of light that will come through the lens or aperture.

Fuzz — light particles rising from the surface of a sheet of paper.

Galley Proof — a continuous sheet of typesetting before being separated into pages.

Gamma — the measurement or contrast in photo images.

Gathering — the placing of printed, folded, signatures in proper sequence.

GCR *(in color separating)* — abbreviation for "**G**ray **C**omponent **R**eplacement". A technique used to remove appropriate levels of cyan, magenta, yellow and replace them with black — usually used to save on ink costs.

Gear Streaks — streaks on a printed sheet spaced the same as the gear teeth on the cylinder.

Generation — the term used for each production stage away from the original.

Goldenrod Paper — a yellow or orange coated paper used to position negatives in stripping, ready for plating.

Gradation — a gradual blending of two colors, color and white, or black and white.

Grain — the direction of the fibers which match the direction of the paper on the paper machine.

Gray Scale *(in photography)* — a series of gradated gray tones which are compared to original copy to show tonal range and contrast (gamma).

Gray Scale *(in photography or desktop publishing)* — the range of gray tones between white and black. A gray scale monitor is capable of displaying distinct gray pixels along with black and white but not color pixels.

Grippers — metal bars that clamp the sheet of paper and controls it as it passes onto the rollers.

Gripper Edge — the front edge of the paper passing through the press.

Gripper Margin — the blank edge of paper which is unprintable and held by the press gripper.

Groundwood Pulp — a wood pulp used in the making of newsprint and publication papers that is mechanically manufactured.

Gum Arabic — one of the ingredients used in the fountain solution on a press to desensitize the areas on a plate so that area will not accept ink.

Gutter — the blank area between the printed area and the binding; also called the inside margin.

Halation — a blurry effect appearing around bright objects or in highlight areas — sometimes resembles a halo.

Halftone — a negative with an image composed of various size dots which have converted continuous tone artwork through a crossline or contact screen.

Hard Copy *(in phototypesetting)* — copy typed on ordinary paper at the same time being put on magnetic or paper tape.

Hard Copy *(in facsimile — fax)* — the original copy of a piece which was sent by a fax machine.

Head Margin — the blank white space between the top of the page and the first line of type or folio.

Hickeys — a blemish on the printed page caused by dirt on the press, dried ink, paper lint, etc.

Highlight — the lightest or whitest part of a photograph which reproduces with the smallest dots or no dots at all on a halftone or color separated negative.

HLS — an abbreviation used to indicate a color model compound of the 3 co-ordinates of **h**ue, **l**uminance, and **s**aturation.

HSV — an abbreviation used to indicate a color model composed of the 3 co-ordinates of **h**ue, **s**aturation, and **v**alue.

Hypo — the short form of the chemical sodium hyposolution which is used to fix the image on photographic film after developing.

Idiot Tape — magnetic tape or unjustified, raw, unhyphenated paper.

Image Setter — a device which transfers a computer image or composition onto phtographic film or paper.

Imposition — the exact position for negatives to be placed so that the page numbers will be in the correct order when the printed sheet is folded.

Impression — the force of a plate, type or blanket applied against the paper.

PARTNERS IN PROFITABILITY

Roosevelt and you!

Make Roosevelt a regular paper source, and add a major player to your sales team!

Roosevelt's experts work with you every step of the way providing the paper you need, whether it's coated or uncoated, rolls or sheets, carloads or skids. They'll get your order to you on time...and they'll quote prices that let you beat the competition without giving up margin! If you want a better bottom line, work with a partner...**call Roosevelt today for samples and prices.**

ROOSEVELT
PAPER COMPANY

Philadelphia (800) 523-3470 ▪ Chicago (800) 323-1778
Cincinnati (800) 354-9829 ▪ Miami (800) 432-3070

Ink Fountain — the part on a printing press that holds and disperses ink to the rollers.

Ink Jet — placing messages or mailing address on exterior or interior pages (i.e. order blank) during the binding process.

Insert — one or more pages printed separately and bound into a book or publication between signatures.

Italic — a slanted style of type which is usually used to emphasize a word or words.

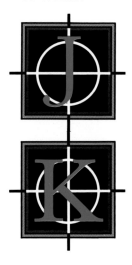

Jog — to form a compact, even pile of sheets of paper.

Justify — to set type so that either or both sides of the lines of type are uniform from top to bottom of the page.

Kerning — moving two characters closer so that parts of their shapes overhang.

Key — the use of symbols, usually letters, to code a dummy to the copy.

Keyboard — the unit which is usually separate from the typesetting unit that inputs and records on magnetic tape or paper.

Keyline — an outline on a finished piece of art to show the exact size, shape, and position for line illustrations or halftones.

Kilobyte — can be indicated by the letters **K**, **KB**; the equivalent of 1024 bytes of digital information.

Knockout — eliminating all background colors surrounding the image which is to print.

Kraft Paper — a brown paper made by a sulfate process using unbleached wood pulp.

Lacquer — the coating applied to a printed sheet for durability or appearance. It is always clear and usually glossy.

Laid Paper — a paper with a ribbed effect produced by a pattern of parallel lines at equal distances.

Lamination — a plastic coating bonded to a printed sheet for durability and appearance by heat and pressure.

Laser Scanner *(four color)* — an electronic machine used to separate color transparencies or reflective art into the four basic process colors, producing negatives for offset color printing.

Laser Scanner *(black and white)* — an electronic machine used to convert continuous tone copy to a high quality finished product regardless of the quality of the copy.

Lay-out *(in paste-up)* — a dummy or sketch to show how the printed piece will appear.

Lay-out *(in platemaking)* — a sheet showing the pattern to be used during the imposing process.

Leaders — dashes or dots in rows across the page to guide the eye.

Letterset — the dry offset printing process which transfers an image from plate to paper using a blanket — versus lithography which requires a dampening system.

Letterspacing — placing a greater space between the letters in a word.

Line Copy — copy which can be reproduced without a halftone screen.

Line Screen — the measuring of a contact screen by the number of lines or dots per inch.

Line Up Sheet — a ruled-up layout base for stripping negatives (also called a master, template, or oil sheet).

Linotronic® — An output device manufactured by Linotype-Hell Co. The machine accepts a disk containing type or images and transforms the information to paper or film.

Logotype — a special design used as a trademark for a company.

Long Ink — ink that flows well on the ink rollers of a press and does not break up into filaments.

Lower Case — the smaller letters versus capital letters.

LPI — abbreviation for "lines per inch" — used to indicate the halftone screen desired ranging from 55-300.

Luminosity — the brightness of color indicated by a value.

Lut — abbreviation for "look-up table" — a table giving the colors which a computer is able to display at a given time. A computer can approximate a color from its available range using this table.

M — the sign used to indicate 1000.

Machine Coating — the coating of one or two sides of a paper on a paper machine.

Make Ready — the setting up of a machine to accomplish a specific chore.

Make Up — arranging lines of text, halftones or illustrations into pages of the correct length.

Mask *(in offset lithography)* — opaque material covering a base flat which is opened in select areas to be exposed on the printing plate, i.e. a mask for blue, another for red.

Mask *(in color separation)* — a negative or positive which is used for color correction.

Master — a word used to describe a ruled layout base for stripping negatives (also called a template, line-up sheet and oil sheet).

Matchprint® — a color proofing system by 3M using colored acetate layers combined to repricate the final product.

Matte Finish — a paper which has no gloss or luster (dull finish).

Matte Print — a dulled finished photo print.

Measure — the width of one piece of type, normally measured in picas.

Mechanical — the board on which the type, photos, and line illustrations are mounted ready for camera.

Megabyte — its abbreviation is "**MB**" — used to indicate the amount of stored data equal to 1024 kilobytes or 1,024,000 bytes.

Middletones — a photograph's tonal range between shadows and highlights.

Misomex® — a machine used to automatically position and duplicate originals to film or plate with very precise register. System picks up original page negatives and masks of varying sizes with vacuum controlled chases, and expose to plates and films up to 58" by 77" in size on a horizontal bed. All aspects of layout and exposure are computer controlled, and require no manual intervention once the pages and masks are stored in order in the film magazine.

Moiré — an unacceptable pattern formed by incorrect screen angles of halftones.

Molleton — a flannel-like, thick, cotton fabric on the dampening rollers of a printing press.

Monitor Calibration — the process of matching chosen colors of printed output by altering the color rendition settings of a monitor.

Monochrome — a display of various shades in one color.

Montage — several photos, placed at angles, overlapping, and cut to various shapes and pasted to one artboard.

Mortise — to trap two screened images together without the use of a line between the two.

EAGLE DELIVERY SERVICE

Let me put your shipments under my wing. Eagle Delivery has the unique systems and professional service that can put savings in your pocket and a smile on your face.

THE EAGLE DELIVERS!

Anything   Anywhere   Anytime

106 Finnell Dr.,Weymouth, MA 02189

617-337-6757   **Fax 617-335-5243**

Mottle — printing which appears uneven or spotty; usually shows more in solid areas.

Mullen Tester — a machine used for measuring the bursting strength of paper.

Mylar® — a mechanically strong and dimensionally stable, polyester material used for stripping negatives; usually used for color or highly illustrated work.

Negative — a piece of film on which the image of the original copy is reversed — the dark areas are white and the clear areas are black.

Newsprint — a paper used by newspaper printers made primarily from ground wood pulp and small quantities of chemical pulp.

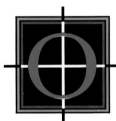

Oblong — a book, magazine, or catalog which is bound on the short side.

Oil Sheet — a ruled-up lay-out base for stripping negatives (also called a master, template, or line-up sheet).

Opacity — the property of paper which effects how much light will be reflected, how much absorbed, and how much will be transmitted through the paper.

Opaque *(in paper)* — the amount of transparency in a paper.

Opaque *(in offset-lithography)* — the elimination of unwanted areas on a negative by painting out.

Opaque Ink — the ink used to eliminate the unwanted areas on a negative.

Opti-Copy® Imposer® System — the Imposer System optically projects transmission or reflective copy into final printing position directly onto platemaking film.

Orthochromatic — photographic surfaces which do not respond to red but do respond to yellow, green, blue and ultraviolet.

Overhang Cover — a cover which is larger than the text enclosed.

Overlay — a transparent sheet placed over the base copy to show another part of the image to print in a different color or black to surprint over a color base.

Overprinting — printing over a previously printed area.

Overrun — the copies which are printed in excess of the requested amount.

Overset — to set type with space in excess of the publications needs.

Packing — the paper placed under the impression cylinder, plate, or blanket of the press to obtain proper pressure for printing.

Panchromatic® — film which is responsive to all visible colors.

Paste Drier — a combination of drying compounds used, a drier in inks.

Paste-up — the board or mechanical with the text, illustrations, or halftones pasted in position for camera.

Pebbling — the embossing of a printed paper to obtain a rippled or pebbled effect.

Perfecting Press — a printing press which prints both sides of the sheet simultaneously.

pH — a number which gives the acid or alkaline value of a solution — 7 is neutral in a scale from 0-14, with the lower value being acid and higher value being alkaline.

Photomechanical — any platemaking process which uses negative or positive film exposed onto plates which have photosensitive coatings.

Pi — mixed type in unusable condition.

Pica — a measurement unit used to measure spaces or lines in printing — 1 pica is equivalent to approximately ⅙ of an inch.

Picking — paper surface which is lifted during printing when the tack or pulling force of the ink is greater than the strength of the paper's surface.

Pigment — the very small solid particles that are used to obtain body, opacity, or color in printing ink.

Piling — the paper coating which accumulates on an offset press blanket, or the ink which accumulates on the offset press plate or blanket.

Pin Register — the placing of special pins on copy, film, composed flats, and plates to guarantee proper register when printed.

Pixel — abbreviation for "picture element" — the littlest distinct unit of a bimapped image capable of appearing on a screen.

If you're tired of being waltzed around by old-technology color separators...

May we have

There's no dancing around THIS issue: Eastern Rainbow has bought FOUR new color-separation scanners since most of our competitors bought their last ONE. Ask around. You'll see.

The client DESERVES the highest level of available technology. While most color separators and printers may claim to offer state-of-the-art scans, what they *really* offer is 1984 (and older) technology. Eastern Rainbow is committed to providing the latest technology color seps. All three of our color scanners are the new generation, 1988-1990 vintage, high resolution, "all digital" variety. Two of them interface with our Chromacom electronic retouching system. In addition, our scanner operators have mastered conventional and "achromatic" techniques. The result is: predictable excellence in color reproduction.

© Corson Hirschfeld

e next dance?

We often refer to our advanced scanning technology as **Choreographed Color**. What better term to describe a color-scanning capability that fully utilizes artistic rendering and technical perfection. That refines detail. That precisely composes each hue, arranges each gradation—so that your color separation is a faithful interpretation of the original. So that it captures the very essence of (or improves) the original transparency. Or, so that it presents a new dramatic rendition of the color transparency—through grainy mezzotint; super-saturated color; or posterization.

Are you keeping step with advanced color scanning? Are your color separations all that they could be? Do they perform well on press? Maybe it's time to consider changing dance partners. Maybe it's time to experience "Choreographed Color." Let us demonstrate the Eastern Rainbow difference. Call us, at (603) 432-2547 or 1-800-258-6228.

Eastern Rainbow, Inc.
Derry Industrial Park, Derry, NH 03038

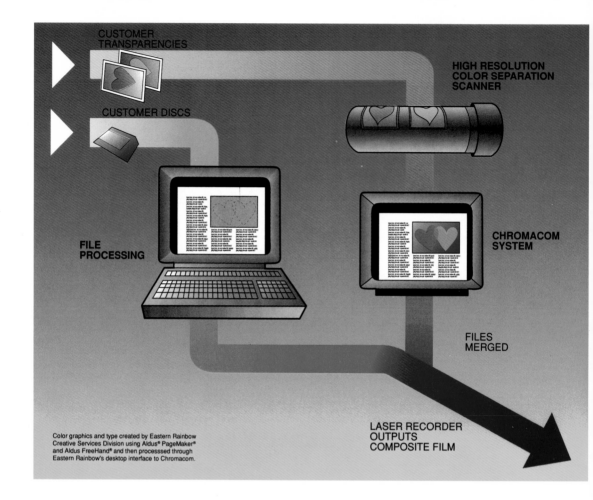

CUSTOMER TRANSPARENCIES

CUSTOMER DISCS

HIGH RESOLUTION
COLOR SEPARATION
SCANNER

FILE PROCESSING

CHROMACOM SYSTEM

FILES MERGED

Color graphics and type created by Eastern Rainbow
Creative Services Division using Aldus® PageMaker®
and Aldus FreeHand® and then processsed through
Eastern Rainbow's desktop interface to Chromacom.

LASER RECORDER
OUTPUTS
COMPOSITE FILM

Great Marriage!

Joining together your Mac generated desktop publishing files and high-resolution color separations should be more than a mere electronic interface.

At Eastern Rainbow, we've arranged it so that excellent matches are made when customers send us their text/graphics discs to combine electronically with our color separations, or to output directly to film. We are very supportive. Newlywed jitters are minimized. Prospects for good communication between both parties and for long-term relationships are excellent. We are very confident in the Eastern Rainbow system for merging desktop computer files with high-

resolution color separations and outputting to film.

Counseling
Our computer graphics technicians offer consultation throughout the business relationship. They'll create complex spot illustrations and graphs where required; or assist in file formatting; they'll even teach you how to strip electronically. Using current software, you'll learn how to strip in tints, create traps and masks. We offer the full AGFA® Professional Type library series (Adobe® Type I) and selected Bitstream® faces. Throughout the courtship, the ceremony and after the honeymoon...our serious commitment is our pledge.

Call for Eastern Rainbow information:
• Capabilities list
• Free subscription to Rainbow Notes color prepress newsletter
• Poster of "rainbow of ballerina legs"

Eastern Rainbow, Inc
Derry Industrial Park
Derry NH 03038
603-432-2547
1-800-258-6228 from Manhatta
and New England (except NH)

Plate — a light sensitive piece of material upon which an image can be recorded — usually metal which in turn is fitted to a plate cylinder on an offset press which then transfers it's image to a blanket which in turn transfers it to paper.

Plate Finish — a smooth, hard finish obtained by calendering the paper.

PMS® — abbreviation for "**P**antone **M**atching **S**ystem® " — a system of ink colors indicated by specific numbers for matching through the use of specific percentages of the process colors.

Point — a measurement used to indicate type size in printing — there are approximately 12 pts. to a pica or 72 points to an inch.

Porosity — the papers property which allows air to permeate; this is an important factor in the penetration of the ink.

Positive — the opposite of a negative — the image on the film is black and the clear area are the white areas on the original copy.

Posterization — making visible steps in a gradation to create a special effect.

PPI — abbreviation for "pixels per inch" — a method of measuring the amount of scanned data.

Pre-press Proofs — any proof made prior to the actual printing process.

Pre-sensitized Plate — a paper or metal plate with a light-sensitive coating.

Press Proofs — a sample of the printed sheet prior to the full production run.

Process Colors — yellow, magenta (red), cyan (blue) with black being the base color. Also written as CMYK.

Process Lens — a highly polished, defective free lens used for line or halftone photography.

Process Printing — offset printing in the 4 process colors.

Progressive Proofs — separate proofs made after the application of each color from the individual color plate.

Proof — a sample of how a photo image or text will appear after printing. They can appear in black and white or color.

Quad — a material shorter than the type for blank spaces used to fill out lines.

Quality Control — checking the consistency of quality by taking and checking sheets randomly during the press run.

Rachwal™ IPM-5000™ (Imposition & Platemaking) System — The IPM-5000 System photographs black and white reflective copy on 70mm roll film, then optically projects it back at full size in any imposition directly onto a printing plate.

RAM — abbreviation for "random access memory" — the memory required by a computer in order to store data which it is processing — this short-term memory disappears when power is shut-off.

Rasterization — the conversion of mathematical and digital data into a series of dots by an image setter in order to produce a film negative or positive.

Ream — 500 sheets of paper.

Recto — righthand side of a page and/or right hand page.

Reducers *(in printing inks)* — any compound which reduces the consistency for printing such as varnish, solvent, or greasy element.

Reducers *(in photography)* — chemicals which reduce the density of the image on a positive or negative or reduces the dot size of a halftone.

Reflection Copy — copy such as photographs which must be photographed by light reflected from its surface.

Reflective Art — artwork ready for scanning or input into a computer.

Register — the exact alignment of two or more images or colors on the same paper.

Register Marks — any sign or mark on the original copy or imposed flats to insure the exact register of text, halftones, or illustrations of two or more colors.

Reproduction Proof — the proof of a type form to be used for photographic reproduction.

RGB — abbreviation for **r**ed, **g**reen, **b**lue — also known as "additive primaries."

Right-angle Fold — two or more folds made at 90° angles to each other.

RIP — abbreviation for "**R**aster **I**mage **P**rocessor" — the part of an output device which rasterizes data in order that it may be put on film or paper.

Roller Stripping — a term indicating that the ink is not sticking to the ink rollers on the press.

Rosette — a pattern which is formed by putting any two screens together at the correct angles.

Rub Proof — an ink which is at its ultimate dryness and will not mar with normal abrasion.

Run-around — an area of type which is adjusted to fit around a picture or design.

Running Head — the book title or chapter heading which is printed at the top of each page.

Saddle Stitch — when signatures of a book are wire-stapled directly into the spine.

Saddle Wire — a book which is bound together by wire going through the centerfold of the pages.

Safelight — a special lamp used in a darkroom to illuminate without fogging sensitized film.

Saturation — the measure of gray in a given color — the saturation being lower when the gray content is higher.

Scaling — calculating the finished size of copy to be enlarged or reduced.

Scan Art® — a black and white laser scanner manufactured by Fuji Photo Film USA, Inc. (see laser scanner).

Sci-Tex® — color electronic pre-press systems for the printing and publishing industry which use digital manipulation and storage of color images.

Score — to mark or crease a piece of paper to facilitate folding.

Screen *(tint)* — a piece of acetate containing rows of gray dots used to tone down a solid color. They are available in different line screens and percentages (dot sizes) to create a wide range of tones with one ink.

Screen *(camera)* — a piece of acetate containing rows of gray or magenta dots (round, square or ellipitical) that is placed over a piece of film on camera when photographing for halftone reproduction. It is available in many different line screens.

Screen Angles — the angled placement of halftone screens to eliminate any moiré pattern — the common angles are black 45°, magenta 75°, yellow 90°, and cyan 105°.

Screen Ruling — the measuring of a contact screen by the number of lines or dots per inch.

Screened Print — a print of a halftone negative.

Scum — a coating of ink printing on the non-image areas of a plate.

Self-cover — a cover which uses the same paper as the enclosed text pages.

Serif — the short cross-lines finishing the main stroke of some letters in many typefaces.

Set-off — the ink on a printed sheet going on to the next sheet as it passes through the press.

Shadow — the darkest part of a picture appearing as the largest dots on the halftone negative.

Sharpen — to lessen in strength, such as halftone dots becoming smaller — the opposite of ''dot spread'' or ''thicken.''

Sheetwise — the printing of one side of a sheet of paper with one plate, turning the sheet over and printing the reverse side with another plate using the same gripper and side guide.

Short Ink — ink that does not flow freely.

Show Through — printing which shows through on the reverse side of the sheet under normal lighting.

Side Wire — to bind a magazine, catalog or book by wiring the sheets or signatures on the side near the spine.

Signature — a form or portion of a form that is bound and folded individually or in combination with other signatures.

Sizing — treating paper to make it resistant to liquid penetration.

Slitting — cutting webs or printed sheets on a press or folder with cutting wheels.

Soft-Dot *(in photography)* — a dot with the halation or fringe around it almost equals the area of the dot itself. The reverse would be a "hard dot" with surrounding area barely noticeable and the dot is very sharp.

Spine — the backbone of a book or space between the front and back covers.

Spiral Binding — wires in a spiral form inserted through punched holes along the binding side of a book or catalog.

Static Neutralizer — a device which eliminates static electricity from the paper to eliminate ink set-off and problems with paper feeding.

Step-and-Repeat — using the same image for stepping to multiple exposures for a predetermined layout.

Stet — a mark or term placed on a proof for correction purposes to indicate something should remain as is.

Stock — the paper or material to be printed.

Stream Feeder — a feeder which feeds more than one sheet of paper, overlapping each other, toward the grippers.

Strike-on Composition — a direct-impression method of typesetting or on a typewriter composing machine (cold type).

Stripping — the placing of negatives or positives on a flat material (paper or plastic) in imposition form for platemaking.

Subtractive Primaries — inks of magenta, cyan, and yellow used to make different colors. These produce darker colors when combined than the additive primaries.

Sulphate Pulp *(in paper manufacturing)* — paper pulp manufactured from wood chips which are pressure cooked in a solution of sodium sulphide and caustic soda.

Sulphite Pulp *(in paper manufacturing)* — paper pulp manufactured from wood chips which are pressure cooked in bisulphite of lime.

Super Calendar — a calendar stack apart from the paper making machine, with alternate metal and resilient rolls, used in producing a high finish on paper.

Surprint — the exposure by contacting of a second negative over the exposed image of the first negative giving a 1-piece negative containing both images.

Tabloid — a publication trim size falling between standard (8½ " x 11") magazines and newspapers. Normally 11" x 16".

Tabloid *(newsprint)* — a newspaper of small format giving the news in condensed form usually with illustrated, often sensational material.

Tabs — indentification usually put along the outside of book for quick reference to material inside.

Tack — the cohesion property between particles; the pulling or separation force of the ink. A "tacky" ink separates and causes picking or splitting of weak papers.

Targa — also indicated by the letters TGA which indicates a file which exchanges 24-bit color files on PCs.

Template — a ruled-up layout base for stripping negatives (also called a master, line-up sheet, or oil sheet).

Text — the body matter of a book or words versus illustrations or headings.

Tints — various strengths or tone areas of a solid color.

Tiff — abbreviation for "**T**aggef **I**mage **F**ile **F**ormat" — a file format which exchanges bimapped images between applications (normally used for scans).

Tipping — an individual page glued into a book.

Tissue Overlay — a thin paper over artwork, used for protection, color breaks, or corrections.

Tooth — the slightly rough finish of a paper which allows it to accept ink readily.

Transparent Copy — illustrative copy which light must pass through in order to be seen, i.e. color transparency.

Transparent Ink — an ink which does not hide the color beneath allowing the under colors to show through. Process inks must be transparent so the colors will blend.

Trapping *(in printing)* — a printed ink which will accept an overprint of another ink.

Trapping *(in desktop)* — allowing abutting colors to overlap to allow for variation in register.

Trapping *(in stripping)* — placing a halftone or illustration film so that it overlaps the base image to insure accuracy on press.

Trim Marks — marks on the copy to show where the edge of the printed page should appear.

Trim Size — size of page after final trim.

Two-Sheet Detector — a mechanism which stops the pick of more than one sheet from feeding into the grippers.

Type Gauge — a tool which measures type in picas.

UCR *(in color separating)* — abbreviation for "**U**nder **C**olor **R**emoval" — A technique used to reduce the combined density of the process colors to insure better control of press gain — usually a maximum of 280% to 320%.

Up — two-up, three-up etc., describes the number of forms to be printed on a larger sheet to make the press run more efficient.

Vacuum Frame — a piece of equipment which is used to expose and contact negatives for dupe film, proofs, or plates while under a pressurized contact.

Varnish — a protective coating applied to a printed sheet of paper cover for appearance or protection.

Vehicle — a liquid component which acts as a carrier for the pigment.

Vellum Finish — a finish on paper that is absorbent allowing fast ink penetration.

Verso — lefthand side of a page and/or lefthand page.

Vignette — an illustration with a background fading away blending into the unprinted paper.

Viscosity — the terminology used to describe the tack and flow properties of ink.

THE POSITIVE SIDE OF THINKING NEGATIVE.

With a reprint program, you can turn those negs in your files into positive profits. Especially when you work with FosteReprints. Our fast, economical service makes it easy for you to fulfill reprint requests from authors, editors and advertisers, in runs from 100 to 50,000. You supply the negatives and tearsheets or mechanicals; we'll provide quality reprints in 8 to 10 days—or faster, with rush service.

It's time to change your attitude about dated film. Think negative; act positive. Call our Sales Department at 1-800-382-0808 for our free reprint kit. And start seeing your old negs in a brand new light.

FosteReprints
800-382-0808

Walk-Off — when part of an image fails to adhere to the printing plate during printing.

Warm Color — a color tending towards the reddish side.

Wash-Up — the cleaning of rollers, plates, and ink fountain of a press.

Web — printing paper in a roll rather than sheets.

Web Press — a press which uses rolls of paper rather than sheets of paper.

Web Tension — the pull or tension which is placed in the direction of the web of paper as it travels through a web-fed press.

Widow — a single word which ends a paragraph alone on a line — not considered good form.

Wipe-on Plate — a plate with a light-sensitive coating which is wiped on or accomplished with a coating machine.

Wire-O Binding — a series of continuous double wire loops running through punched slots on the binding edge of a booklet.

Wire Side — the side of the sheet near the wire in manufacturing — the opposite of the top or felt side.

With The Grain — folding or feeding paper in the same direction or parallel with the paper grain.

Woodcut — an image cut into a plank-grain wood in varying thicknesses — used for making prints.

Work & Tumble — the printing of one side of a sheet, tumbling the paper over from gripper to back using the same side guide and plate to print reverse side.

Work & Turn — the printing of one side of a sheet, turning the paper over from left to right to print the reverse side using the same gripper and plate.

Wove Paper — a soft, smooth finished paper with an unlined surface.

Wrinkles — creases in the paper caused by the press.

Wrong Font — indicated by the symbol "**WF**" to indicate the use of the wrong size or face of type.

Xerography — utilizing a selenium surface and electrostatic forces which forms an image in a copying process.

If you would like to purchase more copies of the *Terminology for the World of Lithography* please send a check or money order for

Each book	$15.00
Shipping & Handling	+ 3.00
Total	$18.00

Substantial discounts are available for quantity purchases. Call for quote.

to: **PPC Publications**
356 South Ave.
Whitman, MA 02382

or call: (617) 447-5522

Name _____ Title _____

Company _____

Address_____

City _____

State _____ Zip _____

Telephone (_____) _____

Terminology

for the

World

of

Lithography

by PPC Publications

(Duplicate order forms accepted.)